BECOMING A PLANT

Natasha Main

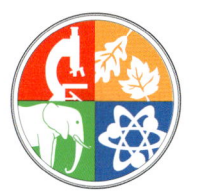

Rosen Classroom Books & Materials™
New York

Flowers, grasses, trees, **shrubs**, and vegetables are types of plants.

Most plants need water and sunlight to grow.

Many plants grow from **seeds** in the ground.

← root

Roots grow from the seed into the ground. They take in water and **minerals** that the plant needs to grow.

← stem

A **stem** also grows from the seed. The stem grows above the ground.

6

The stem carries water and minerals from the roots to the other parts of the plant.

Leaves grow from the stem. The leaves use **energy** from the sun to make food for the plant.

Some plants grow flowers that produce seeds for new plants.

seeds

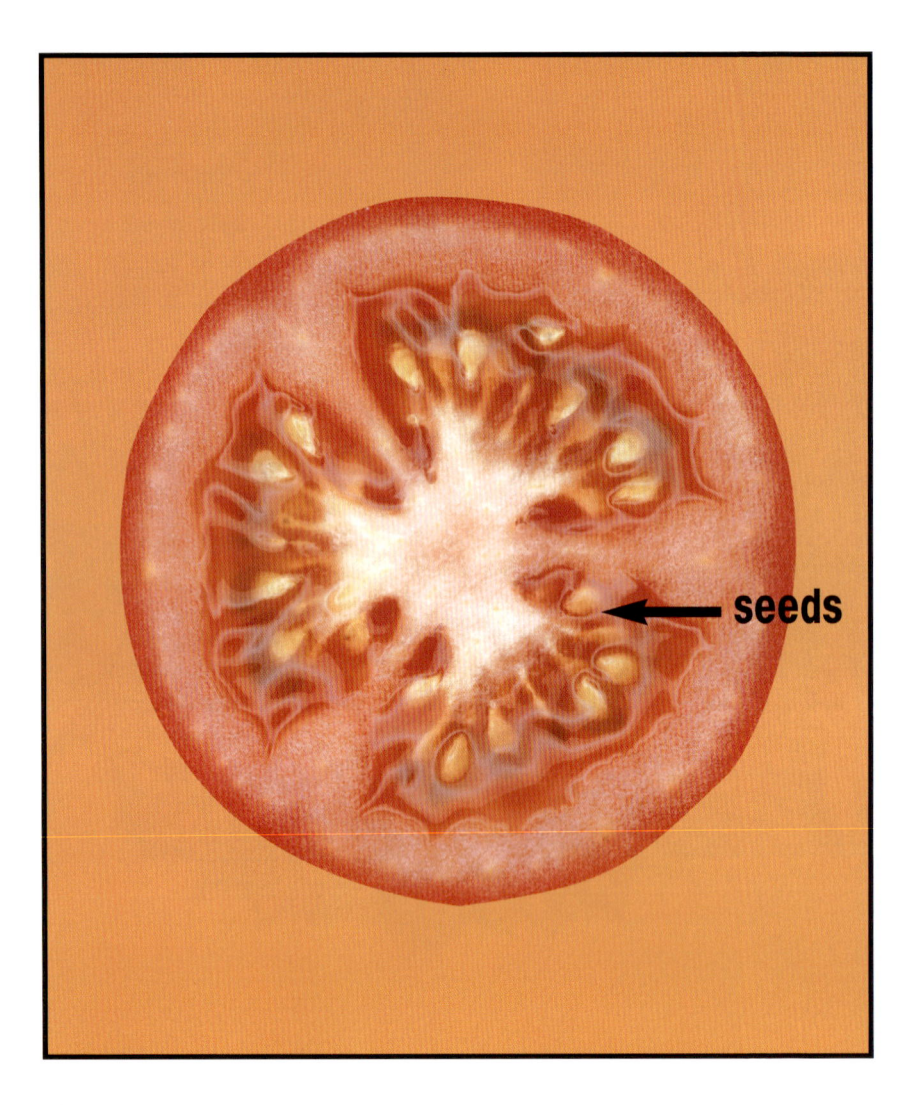

Other plants, such as tomatoes, grow fruit that contains seeds.

Seeds grow into new plants and flowers.

Glossary

energy — Power from a source, such as the sun, that makes things work.

flowers — Parts of a plant that produce seeds or fruit.

leaves — The green part of a plant that grows from the stem.

minerals — Things found in nature that are not animals or plants.

roots — The parts of plants that grow into the ground and take in water and minerals.

seeds — Parts of plants that grow into new plants.

shrubs — Plants or small bushes with woody stems that grow close to the ground.

stem — The part of a plant that supports the plant.